Letang and Julie save the day

By Beverley Naidoo

Illustrated by Petra Röhr–Rouendaal

"An outing! A picnic!"

The words buzzed around Class 3M. When their teacher called for quiet, Letang and Julie could hardly sit still.

"We've done lots of work about our town, so now we shall find out something about the countryside. There's a Country Trail ..." Ms Miller paused.

"Please stop that noise, Michael! We're not on the coach yet."

At playtime, Julie walked outside with Ms Miller.
"I'd better take my wheelie when we go on the Trail, just in case I get tired," Julie said.
"That's sensible," replied Ms Miller. "There's a good path but it is quite a long walk."

On the day of the outing, the class cheered as the coach arrived. "That's the ticket!" said Mr Carter, steadying Julie as she climbed the steps.

Inside there was a scramble for the window seats.
"Hold on a mo!" shouted the driver over his shoulder. "I don't want Piccadilly Circus in here!"
"Calm down!" called Ms Miller. "Have you got your notebooks and pencils?"
"And your packed lunches!" grinned Mr Carter.
The coach revved up and the driver put on some music.
Letang and Julie settled back in their seats.
"It's like in the aeroplane," said Letang. "Ms Miller could be the air hostess!"
Julie giggled and passed on the joke to Sam and Rachel.

At first, the coach kept stopping and starting in the traffic. Then it speeded up, the houses became more spaced out and suddenly there was green everywhere. Julie said softly, "My nan lived in a place like this." "It's very pretty," said Letang. She knew Julie's grandmother had died and that Julie missed her.

9

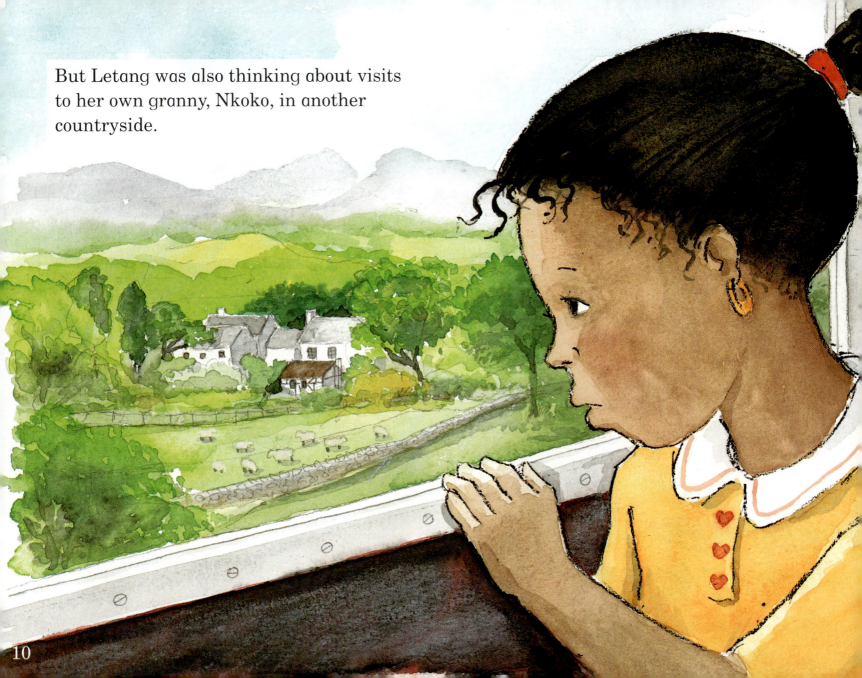

But Letang was also thinking about visits to her own granny, Nkoko, in another countryside.

"We're here!"
The coach had turned off the main road onto a rough track,
shaking everyone inside.
"Look! A river! You didn't tell us about the river Ms Miller!"

The coach stopped close to the stream.
"Surprises are best!" said Ms Miller. "But before any paddling, we are going on the Trail with our notebooks."

Caw! Caw!

A green arrow pointed towards a wooden bridge over the river and into a field of corn.
"I'm hungry!" called out Michael.
"Me too!" added Julie.
"But we've only just started!" laughed Mr Carter.
"My granny grew corn in Botswana and I helped her pound it," said Letang.

There was wheat in the next field.
A flock of crows cawed at them and some children cawed back.
"My dad says they eat mice!" said Michael.
"There are two paths and we can't see any arrows!" called the children who had
gone ahead through a gate leading into woods.

The path Ms Miller chose led out into a large grassy field with some animals grazing near the gate on the far side.
"Cows will be more frightened of you than you of them,"
Ms Miller had told the children earlier.

But as they got closer, the animals began to move towards them.
"Oh dear," said Ms Miller stopping, "they're young bulls!"

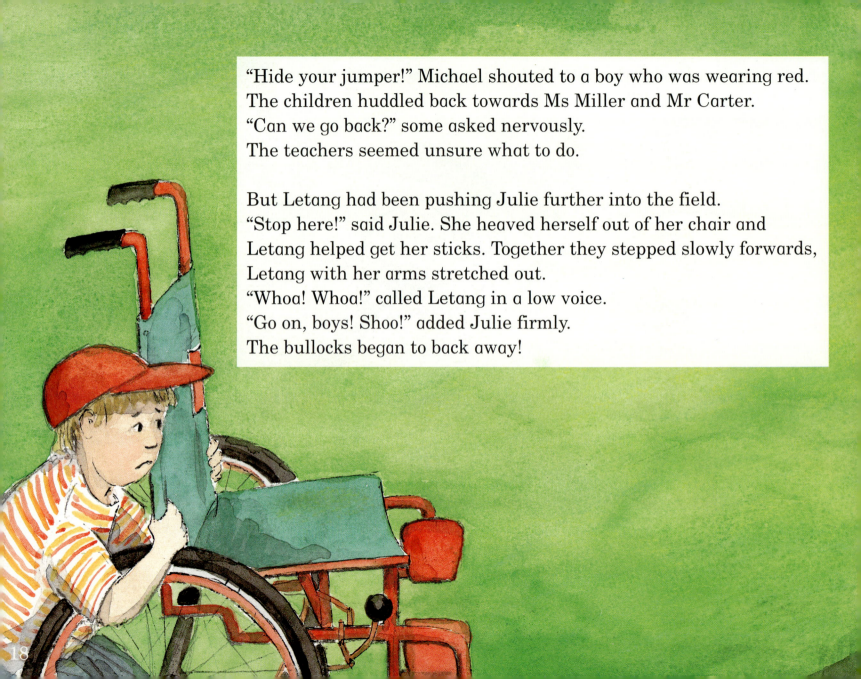

"Hide your jumper!" Michael shouted to a boy who was wearing red.
The children huddled back towards Ms Miller and Mr Carter.
"Can we go back?" some asked nervously.
The teachers seemed unsure what to do.

But Letang had been pushing Julie further into the field.
"Stop here!" said Julie. She heaved herself out of her chair and
Letang helped get her sticks. Together they stepped slowly forwards,
Letang with her arms stretched out.
"Whoa! Whoa!" called Letang in a low voice.
"Go on, boys! Shoo!" added Julie firmly.
The bullocks began to back away!

Children crowded round Letang and Julie on the other side of the gate.

"How come you weren't scared?"

"Who taught you that?"

"Nkoko my granny has lots of cattle and sometimes I helped her," replied Letang, shrugging her shoulders.

"My nan taught me," said Julie, smiling shyly.

"She would have been proud of you!" said Ms Miller.

"It's lucky you two town and country girls were with us! But I shall still write to the farmer to complain!"

It was only a short way back to the bridge.
"I could eat the whole field of corn now!" said Michael.
They tucked into their picnic and afterwards played by the stream.

"My mum will laugh when I tell her what we did!" said Julie on the way home.
"I'm going to ask Ms Miller for a photo to send to Nkoko," said Letang.
"She'll want to see what these English bulls look like!"